for my heart:
russell and dee

Contents

...of de south

...of the Bible folk

...of solace

...of de heart

...of the self

...of de south

a relic
a menaced land
sanctioning a grandsire's
curt southern drawl:
this south

swatting songs
brooms stroke
splintered floors

the blues:
a moaning
yeah!

Ramona Hyman

A Lyric of Oakwood:
For the Enslaved

Go on over there
To that there cemetery
And you'll find the graveyard built on the vision of
That white woman from Maine and sixty-five oak trees
The white woman from Main is a prophet (they say)
And in that grave are the bones of the enslaved
The bones—ain't rattling no more—they all dead.

It is the stories of the enslaved bones
The living folks got to remembering.

The folks got to remembering
How they had paid only slight attention
To the enslaved bones
Got to remembering real good about
Dred Scott—He grabbed freedom
In a place where none was known.

Yeah, the folks got to remembering
Thought about the crabgrass growing
Right on top them bones
Thought about the stories they left behind
All them stories just seeding dirt and grass.

The living folk decided they was going to do something
To pay respects—
To let the self within know the enslaved bones
To sow the lives of them bones in memory.

They built a message board out of stone
Bought some chairs, prettied the place up with
Black-eyed Susans and holly scrubs
And had one of them old time pray meetings

They gathered; it started to rain
As the rain poured down to fertilize the enslaved bones
They raised a song—

In memory of the enslaved bones
And (maybe) the white woman from Maine
They raised a song.
(A song)

Psalms: For the Blues I

If Beale Street could talk
He'd say,

The blues:
Long gone from here

Handy still here though
Made steel by time, white boys,
Winos, dopeheads
Trying to stroll a blues

Ain't none here
'Cause the niggers,
The real funky folks
With sorrow and moaning
For living ain't needed around here
No more

Been moved
Been moved
Along the outskirts of town
To drink whiskey
Underneath the rain

Psalms: for the Blues II

In the rain
We three drag a blues

This blues not
Musicology books about
One strand guitars
And Black boys blowing
Music from soda bottles

This blues is real
It's calluses for hands
Chicken, pig feet, and biscuits
On a Tuesday morning for food

It's real
Like bad feet, corns
And bruised bitten lips

This blues not
Intellectuals arguing
Authenticity in an old
Mississippi upper room

This blues: walking
Down highway 61
To a grave-digging job

It's a dirty boy's lyric
A laundry woman's lament

Ramona Hyman

It's real
Chisels deacons, a church full
Singing gospel songs

Etches deaconess
Chanting. Chanting.

This blues sweeps,
Tryin' to purge a spiritual
In a country back room scene.

A Gathering of Women

(for the four little girls burned in Birmingham)

A story of oak trees
A story of women
Who gather 'round them
To keep watch over
Colored children.

Hear the trees
Rustling the shielding song:

> *Lord—keep at watch over de children*
> *Do remember their names*

The leaves call
The women gather,
To raise the shielding song
For the colored children.

Together they sing:

> *Lord keep at watch over de children*
> *Lord, do remember their names*

One by one
The trees lift toward the sky

One by one
The women lift toward the sky:

Lord, do remember their names

A Sunday morning...
A church...a car...a bomb:
Four little brown girls: *a burning (burning)*

Lord, do remember their names

The trees rustle...rustling:
The women shake their voices
Toward His sky:

(Lord) did you remember their names?

This South I

Angular in vision
Feminine in aura
Masculine in concept
Fundamental in landscape

A pointed land
Language folk speaking
Tongues of a secret ambiguity

(anchored)

On a fragmented landscape

(a canvas)

Layered on a black man's hands crooning
'Cause white boys churning blues from guitars now.

This is the South
Green grass
Stretched like lace along a
Mississippi trail
The men
The women whose slurred speech
Whipped the back of
My grandpapa's papa
My grandmama's mama
Wave to me as if
I am their own

It is a choral of waves
Miscegenated voices
Of boys and girls she milked
Of boys and girls she birthed then sold.

First published in *African American Review*

27.1 (1993): 133-34

This South II

Parlay on a promise
The orange rind feet
Making tracks
Peel sweat
Into my palms

I still see them hanging,
Dried leaves
Dripping from trees

> *death be like life, you know*
> *but turned backwards*
> *like smiling when your heart be frowning*

I still feel them wading,
Swans paddling towards
A Northern star

> *death be like life, you know*
> *but turned backwards*
> *like smiling when your heart be frowning*

I still smell them burning in Mississippi
The stench of people whose graves are etched
In cotton balls
Call out to me
Because I am their own

They tell me:
"wear de South
on your lapel for honor child
I earn it for you."

First published in *African American Review*

27.1 (1993): 133-34

Broken Pieces

The land speaks of them:
Scottsboro boys
The freight train

Trains bring memory

> *boys—havin' fun*
> *mindin' them own-selves*
> *laughin'*

black boys can't laugh
can't mind themselves
down in Alabama

Down in Alabama where white girls tell lies

Trains: bring history

Say them boys rape them girls
They ain't, naw they ain't rape them girls
they just mindin' themselves
laughin'

> *black boys—can't mind them own-selves*
> *black boys can't laugh*
> *can't laugh on trains*
> *'cause trains bring tragedy*
> *down in Alabama*

Ramona Hyman

Down in Alabama where white girls tells lies

Trains—they bring tragedy
Scorching them boys' wings

> *Black Boys can't fly with scorched wings*
> *Down in Alabama*

Trains...

Haiku

Red and white and blue:
She—prodding them to dance the
Dance of "**freedom: now!**"

Ramona Hyman

A Hymn for Montgomery 55

Holy, holy, holy: a hymn of praise
For prophets framing freedom
In Montgomery 55: Strange fruits marching—some
Walking, some crawling—some…

Holy, holy, holy—a hymn of praise
Emptying itself
Americans: black and white; hand in hand
Saintly sighing a freedom song of praise

Holy, holy, holy—the march raises
Into victory: freedom swells, the flag: separate
And unequal shreds into the face of anxious
Soldiers—black and white jumping the broom
Into a new day—the Civil Rights Movement begins

Photograph: For Virginia Durr

I enter your room…
knowing (only)
who they say
you are from
"outside—the inner circle"

books stacked (deliberately) on
the table…telling tales
you know so well…your lips:
a stained glass prism
speak to me…I join
the tender throb of history
in your voice: I walk through it
(*I become it*)

You grow
the American I did not know myself to be
right there
in your voice

Ramona Hyman

For Joann Robinson

I remember Joann mimeographing
Say another black woman been arrested
She say don't ride the bus on
Monday, December 5, 1955

I didn't either, not for 381 days

Bayard Rustin
Standing   outside Montgomery

Waiting:

Nonviolence wills itself into being

Ramona Hyman

Mind Chatter: For Rosa Parks

Her name: Rosa Parks
The day: one
The year: 1955
The month: December
The place: Montgomery, Alabama

Rosa: she tired she say
She tired when she board the bus
Walked down the center aisle—tired,
Sat (in the first of the last ten pairs of seats)
Tired.

Fable go:
> *black folks couldn't ride up front*
> *black folks seats in back of the bus*
> *they just like bugs*
> *sit 'em in the back of the bus so,*
> *tired, tired Rosa—she sit down in the back of the bus*

Bus got crowded
Driver tell black folks sitting
In the first of the last ten pairs of seats
To stand—"make it light on yourselves—*stand!*"

Rosa ain't stand
(ain't make it light)

Fable go:
>**King say:**
>*"Rosa Parks anchored (anchored)*
>*by accumulated indignities of*
>*days gone by, the boundless*
>*aspirations of generations yet unborn."*

>**King say:**
>*"Rosa Parks a victim (a victim)*
>*Of the forces of destiny."*

>**King say:**
>*"When the cup of endurance runs over,*
>*The human personality cries out."*

Rosa Parks, she cry out, she cry
For the black African brought on
A slave ship—packed like sardines in stale water
She cry, she cry out so
I can sit on the bus
She cry; she get arrested
She get fingerprinted
She quiet

Fable go:
>*Nobody know the trouble she see*
>*Nobody know but Jesus*

Rosa Parks tired; black folks tired
She found guilty on 5 December 1955
Black folks tired; they start the boycott
Cause they tired
My mama tired, too
She in the boycott
Yo mama, yo daddy in it, too
They walk. They don't catch the bus
They crawl; they don't catch the bus
They walk. For over a year;
They go to court, keep
Going on to court.

The court get some sense

Fable go:
>*June 1956 Montgomery Court say:*
>*Back of the bus sitting for black folk ain't right.*
>*November 1956 United States Supreme Court say:*
>*back of the bus sitting for black folk ain't right.*

Rosa Parks stopped walking
Black folks stopped walking
White folks stopped walking, too

Rosa Parks get some rest
Black folks get some rest
White folks—they get some rest, too

Martin spoke
I hear thirty-six years   later
The people shouting loud
Do they hear, too?

A Southern Gentleman's Words

For the folks who marched in Selma

you figure—
a scrap of them
got nerve to march
cross Edmund Pettus Bridge in vision
feebly falling.

they was
just some
old black haggard hillbillies
cataloging their right
to vote.

I can't figure them
but it happen
right here in
Selma, Alabama

A Beauty Shop Story:
Thinking of Viola Gregg Liuzzo

It was a Thursday afternoon.
I was sitting in the blue chair at Aunt Dot's Hair Shop
waiting for the girl to wash my hair
when that white woman rose up
in my eyes: Rose up.

I could not get her pale face
out of my brown eyes.
Her face was huge   big-curls-huge
starched in hair spray: Huge.

I sunk down in that blue chair.

Who was this woman?

    A blood relative
    I never made acquaintance with—
    (you know) the kind who show up
    from a long way when a will
    is being passed around the table
    at the family reunion for the one family member
    assigned to do what the legacy commands

I'm sitting in that blue chair at Aunt Dot's Hair Shop
I witness heads being washed
I watch fake hair: snatched out
and all the while I see the white woman—pale
                rising up in my brown eyes.

Who is she?
  I see her
  driving down highway 80. It's dark   night.

She's in a car with the boy.

      Is that Leroy Moton in that car? He scared
                              (they) scared
      knowing freedom coming hearing hate
      roaring up behind them that white woman
      pushing down, down on the gas driving
      seventy miles an hour eighty miles an hour
      ninety miles an hour knowing freedom
      hearing hate shooting into her car.

Leroy sees
Leroy knows
(who done it)

I rise up from the blue chair.
I tell the girl I'll be back for her to wash my hair.
I'm breathing freedom
Cause of the pale woman hanging in my brown eyes

Who she?
A blood relative. An American.

Her name's Viola Liuzzo
And she's dying for my right to vote

Gourmet I

The kitchen
Macaroni, cheese: baking

Mama's laughter hugging cheese and macaroni
the way egg and flour would if mama ain't
love a chicken so well

Mama love the chicken
Say it's not in good taste to use
somebody else's body to bind
(her) macaroni and cheese

She's not one of those animal rights people
Don't t know to be one
though one time she did carry a flag to the march
on Washington with Martin Luther King Jr. and
Uncle Pete
Said she was just demonstrating what Americans do
when things ain't going the way they suppose to

And she did carry a flag up Broad Street during
the Vietnam war: her nephew's legs were blown off
Blowing boy's legs off not necessary
So long as there are mouths to negotiate
(besides) Boys without legs can't stand up to see the stars

Mama's kitchen is a din of laughter on the Lord's day
She fries scallops made from gluten and water
People come by sit at her kitchen table

eat her macaroni, her cheese
chew her scallops made from gluten

They drink lots of water to keep the food from
 lazing around the intestines

And they talk
Medgar Ever's last three words:
Let me go!

Gourmet II

Friday.
preparation day
Mama's in the kitchen
fixing her cream cheese cake
pouring the batter into
a round cake pan
She fixed that cream cheese cake
for Malcolm but with brown
flour Malcolm didn't eat

white (But wasn't the boy from Chicago just trying to
be nice?)

Brain says, (yes)—
Can't be the color of wheat flour
And show nice
In Mississippi

Mama slides the cake in the gas oven
snaps beans at the counter on the
left side of her kitchen on
preparation day
Tulips on the left side
I see Red

Did he know the boy from Chicago murdered for
showing nice?

Ramona Hyman

Hero (A Highway)

Corrida Jones knows the number
folks visit her
play the ten cents hit for forty
sit on her porch laughing summer

Waiting
for winter to wrestle itself from the sky
she buys groceries
for the good times
reads the Bible some twenty-seven ways
she prays:

> *God*
> *George W*
> *Ate peanut butter gave it*
> *history*
> *in Alabama   didn't*
> *help him keep his man*
> *hood I hope he get to your heaven*
> *Cause earth ain't been so fair*

She sleep with an amen on her lips.
Bible cross her chest
She God's woman
got pleasant
posted on
her forehead even though her body
holding pain in her leg:
She Ham's daughter, and George W's sister.

For Fannie Lou Hammer

Fannie Lou's black
breath told how colored had a right
to vote, in a place
that beat her kidneys: they
did not offer her water, either

Ramona Hyman

...of the Bible folk

The Church Folk I

bouquet bonnets (clap)
church, praising—sing them hymns!
lace lyrics hang from
their lips like emeralds (Amen!)

The Church Folk II

pallbearers
of a *savior?*
they pad the pews—their heads nodding
to the sound of Jesus walking through America
feeding children left after their daddies
finished the game

Ramona Hyman

they say God answers prayer
i am still hoping for the answered one
may be it was
not prayed on the right day
at the right hour
in the right room
in the right position

may be to cradle desire in a hand
is not a request

they pray for   her
cut in pieces   (12)
listen to her   body
weeping. to be kept   (whole)

woman
the issue the
blood: the garment
the hem
a touch—
healed

quilting woman
needling their lives:
checkered cotton squares.
where is her man?
a hunting.

Ramona Hyman

Cleansed

Life's in the room:
rules like they talk about in those fancy books best-
selling number ten
don't own meaning here
A sixty-nine-year-old woman from Germany with
raggedy white skin
is trying to walk into living

"Where you going, woman?"
" From life into living," she says
"so long as the brown man with the nice eyes is
my anchor"

The woman from Germany with the raggedy white
skin and the brown man with the nice eyes root a
Bird of Paradise from the ground
The rain starts shedding itself one
drop. Another.
They keep walking
the brown man holding
up the German woman. A
bird of paradise molds a lullaby
in the woman's head. She drops
(to the ground)
The brown man pulls her up into his arms

"This is my life," she says
"a room full
of flower dresses and silver gray wigs."

Your life is more, the brown man says, *more*

The brown man gives her wheat grass and green juice.
She sips, slowly, like a woman taking communion.
She empties her life into living
The brown man with the nice eyes blows: healed

A Prayer for the Dumb

A prayer for the dumb
They who think themselves
"weak in the head."
Who build wooden shacks
Using their hands
Who sit on the side of the road
Selling beans and collard greens
Grown on their
Own plot of land
Who kill chicken and pigs
(Who eat chicken and pigs)
Who birth children too many
Who curse visitors who come too often
But never the sun they curse
But never the rain they curse
But never the storms that ruin white wooden shacks
They build with their hands
Some of them can't read
The books their children
Bring home from school
But they do know how to read
The eyes in need of a friend

A prayer for the dumb
Those who think themselves
"weak in the head"
Who rest themselves
Beside the pond to catch
Its yellow hue in the palm of a hand

They know no thirst
They know how to drink
The life they have been offered without complaint
Their broken teeth and uncombed hair speak:
They do not know the poverty of extravagance
What they do know is they will be with us, always
Their Jesus told them so
Their Jesus told them (so)

Ramona Hyman

shhhhhhhhhhhhhhh
shhhhhhhhhhhhhhhhhhhhhhhhhh:
     the children: praying

...of solace

it hungers

breathes its own sound:

(silence)

War

                         boy's
family—
killed

boy:

    no hands
    to cry
                    inside

when the blind boy speaks
of beauty, sound coils
(a) mimicry of sight

...of de heart

Ramona Hyman

She staggers into dying
"AIDS," folk say
"Took the child's broke soul."

when hurting men cry

earth swells: feel their salient

sounds: rock them into joy

Ramona Hyman

Father

Love
Heaved in a colored man's hand
Christened to stain breath in a daughter's heart.

In medias res

You gathered me into the (pulse)

Of your heartbeat

I lean: he places
his arms around me: closes

himself into me: we are aware

An Old Black Tale:
Seed...Time...Harvest

Looking for a telling story
Found one in family—
My half sister's child

Met her down to the lake
That's where she tell me the story
She say she ain't want to be a nigger woman no more

How she got to be a nigger woman?

She was willed into a nigger woman
The day she started cheating on a man that love her with
a white doctor.
She thought that white doctor was Jesus—
She even bore a baby for that man

Well that's when she got her mind back
She told him they had to end

He told her they would end when he said so
Told her all she would ever be is a nigger woman
(He didn't care if she was ninety-seven years out of
slavery)

That's how we come to be down to the lake
She deposited herself naked before the sky.
She screamed, "leave me go (just you let me go)"

Ramona Hyman

The sky rounded itself
Then opened up—right before us
That sky sucked all the niggerness out of the child
I know it was moving out of her
And into the sky:
Cause what *I* know about niggerness—
It ain't got no color; it just smells real bad.
It was some vile smelling down to the lake that day (*vile*)

Talking about seed...time...harvest

Sorrow seeds into
Ashen silence marching
Noiseless to the center of town:
The old man peering from the bank window yawns:
His story is in our eyes.

...of the self

Paraphernalia for a Suicide: a revelation of life I

(for myself and sonia sanchez)

The mother sat on
the curve of her bed
pitched pennies to woodworks
she spoke:

"What is this sound that
shatters the copper as
I throw it against your womb?"

The daughter lifts her head,
"I have not the nuance to be called woman," she said.

As they spoke, rain rose
to claim the sky. The mother
looked into the daughter's face.

"Have I not taught you
that women are not judged by the
men they encounter nights.
To be woman means you
have felt earth."

"Yes, this is true," the daughter replied,

But,
"a woman who has not smelled her womb
falters in the midst of audiences.

She greets, I am a lonely
asylum: I cannot be amid crows so
long ago she thinks of dying,
of becoming the collage of a cement canvass,
of stepping from the roof."

The mother shook her head like
summer shaking into fall.

"Daughter," she echoed,
"suicide is not a death praised by rivers."

And the daughter stretches
on her sheetless mattress
She feels, she is a reason
to cry, but tears she has been
taught are for rain.

So, she vibrates storms, lightning:
the thunder becomes grave.
She writes,

"Mother,
teach me to harness wind for
you are the herbal fiber
that churns crocodile eyes
and every time I think of
dying, I hear your prayers
bulging from my sides."

First published in *Confirmations: An Anthology of
African American Women Writers* (Marrow Press)

Paraphernalia for a Suicide:
a revelation of life II

I have felt earth—
my own now

Released I am
from asylums

They haunted me:
told me I was made of
rags—torn scattered
used to wipe a beggar's
ashy feet.

Now anchored
by your mumbles woman
I push the halos away
when they come,

(When they come)
I press my palms together
and, well—pray.

Home Bound

1

I remember most:
Front steps of the row house
My head: aching; his lips
Would no longer part to show
The gap in his two front teeth

2

I remember asking:
Why? Did not need an answer
Saw the future hanging:
His mom in a nursing home
His dad (like him, dead)

3

I remember his sister drags a
Foot (lost) in a stroke and the
Boy born on his same day
Gone West:
The sun is suited better for
Laughter there; I remember

4

Him. A casket holding the him
(That did not remain)
I remember
Promising to never
Let him leave my center

Ramona Hyman

Rummaging: A Sanctuary for Myself

on the outside she
smiles—a sanguine smile
look closer (look at her)
when the sun is not in her eyes
when it is almost dark
when the incense has gone out
when the *holy ones* are asleep

she wants to come
into the outer court
she wants to become whole
she has been splintered

     the woman cut into twelve pieces haunts her
     the bungling man swallowed by the whale haunts her

she wants to become whole
she has tried to find heaven
in the wail of a hungry cow
she wants to become whole
but does not know how

she asks the holy men to show her
they do not
they are afraid of mirroring
their own souls to her
(they are afraid of what they will see)

---

she wants to become whole
she has tried to find heaven
in the wail of a hungry cow
she wants to become whole
but does not know how

    the bleeding woman haunts her
    the men with shriveled hands haunt her

she shouts to her holy sisters
bring me into the inner court
they do not
they are afraid of mirroring
their own souls to her
(they are afraid of what they might see)

the holy, holy ones tell her
shhhh—be quiet,
do not be so concerned
with who you are
the sounds you make
they're only sounds—*they say*

she says they are more

    they are her voice

(Her voice is all she owns)
Her **voice** is *all she owns*
Her voice-is—
All she owns

A legacy
A bequest to
Devote healers of scabs
Within the tribe:
A southern narrative

About the Author

Ramona L. Hyman is an Assistant Professor of English at Oakwood College. Her writing has been included in journals and anthologies, such as *African American Review* and *Confirmations: An Anthology of African American Women Writers* (Marrow Press). Hyman has also served as a speaker for the Alabama Humanities Foundation. She lives in Huntsville, Alabama.